Arthur Weir

The Romance of Sir Richard

Sonnets, And Other Poems

Arthur Weir

The Romance of Sir Richard
Sonnets, And Other Poems

ISBN/EAN: 9783337007263

Printed in Europe, USA, Canada, Australia, Japan

Cover: Foto ©Thomas Meinert / pixelio.de

More available books at **www.hansebooks.com**

THE ROMANCE

OF

SIR RICHARD

SONNETS, AND OTHER POEMS.

BY

ARTHUR WEIR, B.A.Sc.

AUTHOR OF "FLEURS DE LYS AND OTHER POEMS"; LATE SECRETARY OF
THE SOCIETY OF CANADIAN LITERATURE, MONTREAL; HONORARY
MEMBER OF THE SAME, AND MEMBER OF THE HALIBURTON
SOCIETY, WINDSOR, NOVA SCOTIA.

MONTREAL:
WILLIAM DRYSDALE & CO., PUBLISHERS.
1890.

TO MISS LOUISE SKEAD.

As, in old time, the tempest-scorners set
   Their ship's keen prow into the golden rain
   Of eve, and ventured o'er the unkeeled main
To under lands, and myriad dangers met
From savage hordes and coasts the waves that
    fret ;
   That they might gold and sunborn gems obtain
   For their belovèd Queen, her smiles to gain,
And her thanks won, their hardships did forget:

   So I have ventured over thought's vast seas
     Into the land of visions, deeming sweet
       Long hours of sunless toil, if I might reach,
     And bring, as my love-tribute, to thy feet,
       At last, the gold of thought and gems of
         speech,
   Paid by thy thanks, Imperial Louise.

CONTENTS.

THE ROMANCE OF SIR RICHARD.

	PAGE
Prologue	1
The Vigil	4
The Tournament	7
Epilogue	9

OTHER POEMS.

The Sun Worshippers	11
On the Shore	15
A Christmas Carol	20
A Snowshoe Song	22
Premises and Conclusion	24
Faded Violets	27
A Christmas Lullaby	31
Destiny	34
The Valedictorian	37
The Lilacs and the Star	48
Christmas	49
The Flirt	50
Love and a Sermon	52
A Pair of Geese	55
The Woodbird	58

CONTENTS.

Tell Me, Dearest, Why?	60
Death Comes to Us All	62
Little Miss Blue Eyes	63
In Love's Bowers	64
In Exile	66
Not Nature, but Man	68
To Her Lover	70
The Flower Girl	71
To a Coquette	72
A Song	73
Intimacy	74
The Courier de Bois	75
Iscariot	76
Come Down to the Shade	77
Love	78
The Maiden's Song	79
To Rose	80
Mind and Body	82

SONNETS.

To Louise	83
Albani	84
In the Morning	85
I Had Been Like a Ship	86
The Eternity of Life	87
The Pearl Bracelet	88
The Blind Street Fiddler	91

CONTENTS.

How Shall I Paint Thee	92
Christ Was No Idler in Luxurious Halls	93
Night Thoughts	94
To the Sea	95
If You Should Die	96
Anticipation and Realization	97
Fear Not to Do Right	98
Why a Bride Weeps	99
The Noblest Poem	100
My Lady	101
The True Immortals	102
The Pantheist	103
In the Canoe	104
Sonnets at Niagara	106
Be Thine Own Image Builder	111
Heart Hunger	112
Dante to Beatrice	113
Cupid and Psyche	114
A Mother's Thought	116
At the Recital	117
Heine's Three Kisses	118
Epilogue	121

THE ROMANCE OF SIR RICHARD;

SONNETS AND OTHER POEMS.

THE ROMANCE OF SIR RICHARD.

Prologue.

By brake and bower, by fen and field,
   And lakes that gemmed fair Nature's breast;
With shadowy lance and silver shield,
   Came riding Night upon his quest.
The stars in countless myriads glowed,
   Like jewels, in his sombre helm,
And earth grew silent as he rode
   Again through his reconquered realm.

The Wind, his unseen trumpeter,
   Gave challenge to the recreant Day.
There was no answer, save the stir
   Of leaves, that turned to see the fray.
No answer; and the wind was still,
   And all the leafage fell asleep,
While Night rode slowly up the hill
   Into the ruined Norman Keep.

O'er pointed arch and crumbling wall,
   In tangled wildness swept the vine,
And in the empty banquet hall
   In flower cups swam the dew, for wine.
A moonbeam, like the torch of Fame
   That dissipates oblivion's gloom,
Fell on a sculptured knight, whose name
   One still could read upon his tomb.

What lover's fancy ruled our brains
   That we should seek the ruined hall,
And listen for the minstrel strains,
   Were wont to cheer the vassals all?
Why, stealing from the lighted room,
   The merry laugh, the graceful dance,
Sat we with Night beside the tomb
   To speak of days of shield and lance?

The only minstrel was the owl,
   The only vassal was the bat;
The shadows, like gaunt monks in cowl,
   Stood round the place wherein we sat;
And, while my shoulder propped thy head,
   Thy fair hand put the vines aside,
And I, in quaint, old metre, read
   How brave Sir Richard lived and died.

"He was a noble Christian knight,"—
 So wrote the long-forgotten bard,—
"A doughty champion of the right,
 His lady's smile his best reward.
This earnest follower of the Cross
 At Hierusalem was slain :
Erst Merrie England mourns his loss,
 Nor e'er shall see his like again."

So fair the night, so deep our love,
 So sweet the joy of solitude,
We stirred not from the tomb, but wove
 Sir Richard's romance as we would.
"The lady fair am I," saidst thou,
 "Sir Richard, dearest, shalt thou be,
As well would Richard mine, I trow,
 As he for his love, fight for me."

Then played we twain a mimic play,
 (And in the moonlight deemed it real),
Of bygone days of chivalry,
 Fair dames and knights in burnished steel.
I told how lonely watch I kept
 One night—that same pale moon above—
And thou at jousting how I swept
 The lists, and crowned thee Queen of Love.

The Vigil.

He Speaks.

All day the courtyard teemed with men,
    All day the tinkling hammers rang,
All day, from many a windy den,
    Skyward the ruddy forge fires sprang.
The day it was before the tilt,
    And swarthy armourers showered their blows
On lance and shield, on blade and hilt,
    From dawn till night-dews washed the rose.

The king was come, with all his court,
    The tourney with his smile to grace;
Perchance to break a lance in sport,
    Or clothyard in the white to place.
All England's noblest knights were there,
    Each eager in the lists to prove
His skill, and crown his lady fair
    The Queen of Beauty and of Love.

Darkly the moated waters swept
    Around the castle's massive pile,
The night when I my vigil kept
    Of knighthood in this gloomy aisle.

The yew tree tapped the tinted panes,
   The sad owl hooted in the glade,
And Philomel, in plaintive strains,
   Her secret to the night betrayed.

Midsummer lightnings, sweetly shy,
   Low in the far horizon burned,
Like love-light in thine azure eye,
   When mine upon thy face is turned.
And as amid the gloom I stood,
   With the departed great, alone,
A moonbeam through the solitude
   Came creeping on from stone to stone.

I pondered on the glorious dead,
   And on the greatness of my race;
And where the moonbeam lay I read
   How one chose death before disgrace.
Then, as the light crept softly by,
   I conned the legends, one by one,
And vowed that, unto death, would I
   Of noble sires prove worthy son.

I thought upon the knight's estate
   I was to enter on the morn,
His love of truth, of wrong his hate,
   His pity for the feeble born.

I thought how ready was his blade
  To set Oppression's victim free;
And then my fondest thoughts, sweet maid,
  As steel to loadstone, turned to thee.

Companion of my boyhood hours,
  Thy memory cheered me in the gloom,
As the rich scent of scattered flowers
  Of half its sorrow strips the tomb.
Methought thou wast beside me there,
  Within the dimly-lighted aisle,
Thy voice on the enamored air,
  The shadows routed by thy smile.

Methought I heard thy bird voice say:
  "Hold fast to every noble thought,
And as this night shall end in day,
  So shalt thou unto God be brought."
Methought thou gav'st me words of cheer,
  Methought I felt thy shy caress,
And duty shone before me clear,
  While vanished sin and wretchedness.

Then suddenly the risen Sun
  Stood radiant on the marble floor;
The night its shadowy course had run:
  At last, my lonely watch was o'er.

I left the precints of the dead,
    And to the dewy courtyard passed,
Before the king to bow my head,
    And rise Sir Richard, knight at last.

The Tournament.

She Speaks.

Throughout thy dreary watch-night, love,
    I sat within my turret room,
And prayed the Heavenly Lord above
    To guard thee in the charnel gloom.
I saw the moonbeam, as it crept
    To light the sculptured legendry,
And envied it, because it kept
    A night-long vigil, dear, with thee.

When laggard morning came at last,
    And thou, in glittering war array,
Cam'st, summoned by the trumpet blast,
    To combat in the mimic fray.
I went to see thee at the tilt,
    And, though I knew how strong thine arm,
To cheek my warm blood played the jilt,
    For fear that thou shouldst suffer harm.

I saw the king the signal give,
   I saw thee spur against the knight,
I shrieked: "They cannot meet and live!"
   And veiled mine eyes to hide the sight.
But when uprose the vast concourse,
   One-minded in its praise and mirth,
I peeped. Unharmed, upon thy horse
   Thou wast, thy foeman borne to earth.

And ever, as the day wore on,
   Thou hadst, methought, a charmèd life,
For of the doughtiest knights was none
   Could overcome thee in the strife.
Thou wast as moveless as a rock
   That, compassed by an angry sea,
Undaunted meets its fiercest shock,
   And hurls it back confusedly.

The day was drawing to its end,
   And Night was tilting with the Sun,
When thou before the king didst bend
   And take the crown that thou hadst won.
Adown the lists I saw thee ride;
   One instant did our fond eyes meet,
And then of England's knights the pride
   Laid the gold trophy at my feet.

THE ROMANCE OF SIR RICHARD.

Epilogue.

"What said the king?" I, laughing, cried.
 "Did he not take thee by the hand
And say, if I was England's pride,
 Thou wast the fairest in the land?
And, when uprose the smiling sun
 Upon my first of happiest days,
Did he not see us twain made one,
 And loud as any cry thy praise?"

'Twas thus Sir Richard's life we wove,
 And brought it to a happy end,
For happy lovers ever love
 All other lovers to befriend.
Then ere we from our idyl turned,
 I, as befits a poet true,
From what of knighthood we had learned
 A moral for the present drew.

I said: "We still have knights as great
 As those who fought that tourney morn
Who love the truth, hold wrong in hate,
 And pity show the feeble born.

Still lends the faithful knight his aid
   To set Oppression's victim free,
And in his soul some lily maid
   Still whispers : " Seek nobility."

We rose in silence from the tomb,
   Scarce needing speech our thoughts to share,
And slowly from the castle gloom
   Passed out into the midnight air.
Arm twined in arm, and souls linked fast,
   We sought the revellers again ;
While Night kept vigil with the Past,
   Each happy in its own brief reign.

THE SUN WORSHIPPERS.

Not mindless they who kneel before the Sun,
    And build their temples on cloud-shaming hills,
To catch its latest beam when day is done,
    Its earliest when the misty morning fills
    The air with melody, and babbling rills
Among the hillside groves begin to gleam,
    And every flower its odors sweet distils.
Not mindless they who hold the Sun supreme,
But seekers after truth, who find it in a dream.

Indeed, not mindless they the Sun who deem
    Giver of life to earth, and air, and sea,
Though to the ignorant mind they mad may seem;
    For, blinded by the Godhead's majesty,
    Before His noble work they bend the knee
In worship, but one step from Him astray.
    Who knows if nearer other faiths may be,
Whose followers to departed heroes pray,
And look on God as but a mightier man than they!

Seaward no wandering streamlet sings its way,
   No zephyr stirs the leafage, not a flower,
Fanned by the humming-bird, blooms on its spray,
   But owes its birth and life to the Sun's power.
   No mushroom growth upsprings within the hour,
No century-living oak mounts to the skies,
   No harmless lizard dallies in a bower,
No wild beast lives, no bird, no insect flies
But that the Sun strength for its daily life supplies.

It is the Sun that lights the maiden's eyes,
   Beats in her veins, and rounds each glowing charm ;
For every thought a sunbeam lives and dies ;
   It is the Sun that nerves the hero's arm,
   That peals the vesper bell and war's alarm.
The sentinel, that through the rayless night
   Guards the beleaguered garrison from harm,
Has drawn his power to watch from the Sun's might,
Nay more, it is the Sun that taught his sword to bite.

No act, no thought, no sorrow, no delight,
   No life, no death, stability, nor change,
No deed of wrong, no battle for the right
   But to the Sun we trace. Throughout the range
   Of time grown grey and time unborn, the strange
Vicissitudes of earth are through the Sun.
   The fossil past has stored, as in a grange,
His beams to feed the ages yet to run
Till earth grow cold in death, and time, at last, is none.

The warmth that glows within the grate was won
   Long æons since, ere man to breathe began,
By graceful tree ferns from the powerful Sun.
   At the Sun's call the icefields over-ran
   The earth, and slew well nigh all life but man.
The earth itself was born in the Sun's breast,
   And when in death it waxeth cold and wan
Will turn again, and, like a child distressed,
Upon that bosom fall, and find eternal rest.

Not mindless, then, are they who have confessed
   The Sun their God, and on cloud-shaming hills
Have built their temples that at eve the west,
   At morn the east with glorious radiance fills.
   Not mindless they whom the Sun's grandeur thrills
With worship, though they know not the Unknown
   Who rules the Sun, and earth through it instils
With greatness : these fanatics not alone
Worship for God the brilliance which obscures His throne.

ON THE SHORE.

Robed in summer's golden splendor, jewelled by
  the tinkling waves,
  Many a crescent promontory takes the sea in
    its embrace.
Starfish cluster on the sand-plains, crawfish lurk
  among the caves,
  Where the seaweed's rippling tresses interlace.

Childlike, clings the shimmering sunlight to the
  bosom of the sea,
  Lulled to slumber by the crooning of the
    waves upon the shore ;
And beyond the purpled islands, like a seagull
  winging free,
  Slips a yacht, and fades from sight for ever-
    more.

With its shadowy hand a pine tree gathers
  sunbeams from the ground,
  Drops them, harkening to the wind's tale,
    then upgathers them anew ;

Dusty brown, the ripe grass whispers on a high sea-fronting mound,
  Flashing emerald when the sea wind wanders through.

In and out among the gneisses, peering in their chinks and caves,
  Strays a dawn-eyed child whose footsteps scarcely stir the mobile sand ;
While the sunbeams smile upon her, and the lithe, foam-crested waves,
  Doglike, fawn and leap to kiss her slender hand.

From the far sky's hollow portals glide vast billows to the shore,
  Bearing oft a briny treasure to beguile the eager maid ;
Now a trailing vine that drooped once some lithe-limbed sea-maiden o'er,
  As she sat and combed her tresses in its shade ;

Now a piece of sodden driftwood, of some unknown ship a part,
  From the waste of beryl waters, trending landward many days

ON THE SHORE.

With its tale of storm and shipwreck, making
    sad the maiden's heart,
  And her merry eyes grow thoughtful as they
    gaze.

Questioning, she turns to ocean, which, with
    snowy breast laid bare
  To the amorous rocks, with kisses winds its
    arms about its love ;
And she wonders that the heart which throbs
    beneath that bosom fair
  Should so cruel in its hour of anger prove.

Questioning, she hears the love song chanted by
    the dallying breeze,
  As it wooes the graceful pine tree in the
    shadows on the height,
And she wonders how the voice that daily sings
    such songs as these
  Can to death lure helpless seamen in the
    night.

Something rarer claims her fancy; she forgets
    the wreck and wind
  As she looks on the reflection of her own
    young, happy face

In a wave that, oversleeping on the beach, was
    left behind
  By its comrades, in a hollow rock's embrace.

Then she wreathes the tiny sea shells in a
    many-tinted chain
  Round her neck, or, like a mermaid, inter-
    weaves them with her hair,
Till she seems a child of Ocean, who shall sink
    from sight again
  With the foam wraiths that from sharp rocks
    rise in air.

Oft she finds a pearl-lipped sea-shell, turns it in
    her slender hand,
  Drains its little ocean from it, setting its weird
    music free,
Listens while it sings the songs with which the
    Ocean charms the strand,
  Till she tires, and throws it back into the
    sea.

Then she stoops to gather pebbles, and around
    her shoulders fall,
  As a golden cloud at day-death veils the sun,
    her wayward locks;

And her voice finds birth in laughter at the
  startled crabs that crawl
 From her pathway to their caverns in the
  rocks.

Nature's book upon the sea-shore is for her a
  wondrous tome,
 And she reads its fairy stories with an ever
  new delight,
While Old Ocean turns the pages with his finger-
  tips of foam,
 And on silent wing the happy hours take
  flight.

A CHRISTMAS CAROL.

Whither wend ye, wise kings three ;
  Whither wend ye
With your perfumes and your gems,
Fit for princely diadems ;
  Whither wend ye ?

Whither wend ye, wise kings three ?
  " O'er hill and lea,
Where yon star, that, bright and high,
Through the azure of the sky
  Leads constantly."

Seek ye what, O ! wise kings three ;
  For what seek ye ?
Seek ye wealth, or seek ye power ?
Sup ye here and rest an hour,
  Road-worn ye be.

" Not for riches wander we,
  Nor sovereignty ;
Nor can wait to sup and rest :
Of a king we are in quest,
  We wise kings three.

"For a mighty king seek we,
    Born lord to be
Of all kingdoms of the earth.
Canst thou tell us of his birth,
    Where dwelleth he?"

Yonder in a manger, see!
    There lieth he;
For, the humble place above,
Shines the star, and doth not move:
    There must he be.

"'Glory unto God,' sing we
    Glad wise kings three.
Spice and jewels shall we bring
To the cradle of the king,
    Our gifts to be.

"'Unto God all glory be,'
    Thus sing will we;
For, our weary journey done,
We may rest and sup, each one,
    Joy'd wise kings three."

A SNOWSHOE SONG.

Hilloo, hilloo, hilloo, hilloo ;
Gather, gather ye men in white ;
The wind blows keenly, the moon is bright,
The sparkling snow lies firm and white :
Tie on the shoes, no time to lose,
We must be over the hill to-night.

Hilloo, hilloo, hilloo, hilloo ;
Swiftly in single file we go,
The city is soon left far below.
Its countless lights like diamonds glow,
And as we climb we hear the chime
Of church bells stealing o'er the snow.

Hilloo, hilloo, hilloo, hilloo ;
Like winding sheet about the dead.
O'er hill and dale the snow is spread,
And silences our hurried tread.
The pines bend low, and to and fro
The maples toss their boughs o'erhead.

Hilloo, hilloo, hilloo, hilloo ;
We laugh to scorn the angry blast,
The mountain top is gained and past.

A SNOWSHOE SONG.

Descent begins, 'tis ever fast,—
A short quick run, and toil is done.
We reach the welcome inn at last.

Shake off, shake off the clinging snow,
Unloose the shoe, the sash untie,
Fling tuque and mittens lightly by.
The chimney fire is blazing high,
And, richly stored, the festive board
Awaits the merry company.

Remove the fragments of the feast!
The steaming coffee, waiter, bring.
Now tell the tale, the chorus sing,
And let the laughter loudly ring.
Here's to our host, come drink the toast,
Then up! for time is on the wing.

Hilloo, hilloo, hilloo, hilloo;
The moon is sinking out of sight,
Across the sky dark clouds take flight,
And dimly looms the mountain height.
Tie on the shoes, no time to lose,
We must be home again to-night.

PREMISES AND CONCLUSION.

The breath of summer stirred her hair,
   And swept a tress athwart his cheek,
And as his warm blood met it there
   He had it in his heart to speak;
For something in the shy caress
   Of that gold ringlet unconfined
Filled him with longings to possess,
   And whispered that the maid was kind.

An open book upon her knee
   With fluttering leaves her fingers fanned.
It was no ornate poesy,
   No novel from a master hand.
It taught of science' wondrous lore,
   And unto strange conclusions led,
The volume they were bending o'er,
   That youth and maiden, head to head.

She read: "Brute animals are mere
   Machines, devoid of consciousness;
They do not love, nor hate, nor fear,
   Experience pleasure nor distress:

And man, no more than this is he,
  Let him not boast his intellect ;
In thought, in act he is not free,—
  External forces him direct."

She closed the book, and veiled her eyes.
  Soft lashes wooed each downy cheek.
He gazed and thought: "From Paradise
  Surely the sprites a truant seek."
Then spake the maiden, dreamily,
  And asked ; "Can these stern words be true ;
Are we automata, or free
  Or good or bad to know and do?"

Gently he answered (still the tress
  Against his cheek, they sat so near):
"What mere brutes are we can but guess
  Yet with ourselves the truth is clear.
The love for thee within my heart,
  The joy I know when thou art nigh,
Are not a paltry, force-ruled part
  Of some complex machinery.

"The love of mother for her child,
  The creed of an eternal soul,
Such traits cannot be reconciled
  With credence in mere force-control.

What force, external to the mind
   Can cause sublime self-sacrifice?
Ah, no! methinks that human kind
   Is not some well-made, dead device.

"And yet,"—the tress against his cheek
   Made his erst timid heart grow bold—
"Even at this moment, as I speak,
   By beauty's force I am controlled:
A mere automaton am I,
   Obedient to Dame Nature's laws,
And if I kiss thee—thus—dear, why,
   Thou shouldst not blame me, but the cause."

FADED VIOLETS.

Do you remember these blossoms you tost me—
   Violets once, but now formless and grey—
In those bright days when my heart was first
    lost me—
That's what the sight of your loveliness cost me—
      Do you remember them, pray?

No? Now, that's strange; I was sure you'd
    remember.
   Dear, think again : 'twas a midsummer night.
Red shone the moon through the trees, as an
    ember
Glows through the grate bars in frosty December,
      Cheerily shedding its light.

Over the arch of each lightly-clad shoulder
   Flowed your white wrap. You'd these flowers
    at your breast.
Warm though the day was, the night had grown
    colder ;
Zephyrs had wakened, and, in the dusk bolder,
      Softly your tresses caressed.

Then I said something. Absurd? That's undoubted,
    Grudging the buds their unmerited bliss,—
Love reigns by starlight and caution is routed;
Lips smile at words that by day would have pouted;
        Starlight was given for this.

Nothing you answered, but just as we parted,
    You in the doorway and I on the path,
Shyly you tossed me the nosegay, and darted,
Into the house, while I stood, happy-hearted,
        I who had feared for your wrath.

Now you remember! What, nothing whatever,
    Love! and you ask—with the buds lying here—
How I remember? Forget will I never.
Why? Well, a tale, though at tales I'm not clever,
        Best makes my meaning appear.

Into the cleft of a cliff, thunder-riven,
    Where a stream gurgles o'er mosses and rocks,
Chased by the sun, at day dawning are driven
Out of the star-blossomed pastures of heaven,
        Night's silent, shadowy flocks.

Here, with the spray of the stream in its chalice,
  Dwelt a shy blossom and swayed in the
      breeze.
Beetles and ants through its pistilate palace
Wandered at will, and beslimed it in malice,
    While stole its nectar the bees.

Ever the dun cliffs the daylight denied it ;
  Only by shadows it knew of the sun ;
Moaning, the streamlet flowed darkly, beside it,
With but its yearning for ocean to guide it ;—
    Joy in that cleft there was none.

Once came a day in the life of the flower
  When slid the sun, like a bird, o'er the cleft,
Flooded the blossom with light for an hour,
Then passed away to his occident bower,
    Leaving the poor plant bereft.

Yet that short hour left remembrance behind it;
  Gaily the plant put forth blossoms anew,
And, though the gap's jealous walls still con-
    fined it,
No more the clustering shadows could blind it,
    For the sun seemed to shine through.

Phœbus, the day king, forgot, or knew never,
  How glad he made a life bitterly drear,
There, that's my tale. You can guess, if you're
      clever,
Why in my bosom I carry forever
      Violets scentless and sere.

A CHRISTMAS LULLABY.

The restless clock is ticking out
   The hours that go before the dawn,
And icy moonbeams dart about
   The snow that shrouds the slumbering lawn,—
The lawn that Santa Claus must cross
   Ere he shall reach my baby's cot,—
Ah! who shall measure Bertie's loss
   Should Santa Claus come not!
        Sleep, softly sleep, my pretty one;
           I hear the neighing of the steeds,—
        Good Santa Claus has just begun
           His round of kindly deeds.

What has the little man for thee,
   My precious babe who slumb'rest there?
He brings, sweet one, a gift from me,
   A mother's love, a mother's care,—

A mother's care that shall not wane,
  While hands can toil or brain can think,
Until that day shall come again
  When thou shalt cross life's brink.
      Sleep, softly sleep, my pretty one ;
        I hear the neighing of the steeds,—
      Good Santa Claus has just begun
        His round of kindly deeds.

He brings a cross, he brings a crown,
  And places them on either hand.
Upon the cross thou must not frown,
  For some day thou shalt understand,
Shalt understand the preciousness
  That to the sombre cross pertains,
And thou wilt hold the crown far less
  Than of the cross the pains.
      Sleep, softly sleep, my pretty one ;
        I hear the neighing of the steeds,—
      Good Santa Claus has just begun
        His round of kindly deeds.

He brings the greatest gift of all
  In bringing thee this Christmas Day.
The deathless love it doth recall
  Of Him who took thy sins away ;

A CHRISTMAS LULLABY.

And when no more thy mother's care
  Can guide thy footsteps, Baby Mine,
Thy steps shall be secured, eachwhere,
  By love of One divine.
      Sleep, softly sleep, my pretty one ;
        I hear the neighing of the steeds,—
      Good Santa Claus has just begun
        His round of kindly deeds.

DESTINY.

A fledgeling swung within a wind-blown nest,
Deep cradled in a modest hawthorn crest.
  To peer at it the curious leaves bent over,
And crooned shy songs to lull it into rest.
  The mother bird sang to the sun above her,
Till stirred the gold air, throbbing like her breast,
    With love expressed.

Through summer days, the running sands of years,
Shadow and sunlight crossed protecting spears,
  Ebon and gold, above earth's tender guest.
With eager lips the leafage drank the tears
  Of weeping clouds, lest it should be distressed,
And mother love sang in its listening ears
    To soothe its fears.

Frail as a crystal flake of breast-white snow,
And fearful as the echo-fleeing doe,
  Weak as the wayward thistledown which veers

In winds that cannot bow the daisy low,
   Instinct with charms born of more heavenly
      spheres,
The little nestling, in the summer glow,
      Swung to and fro.

Thus, wind-nursed, passed its youth ; and then
    my love
Found the shy nest within the hawthorn grove,
   And dowered the bird with all love could
      bestow.
I heeded not the warning poised above
   In heaven's blue arch, nor fateward turned to
      know
That the frail nestling would its pinions prove,
      And skyward rove.

Days wing the soul and poise it for its flight ;
Days give it strength to win life's azure height.
   With lapse of days the feeble fledgeling throve,
And dreamed sweet dreams that thrilled it with
      delight.
   Then while, soul-sick, I watched, its young
      wings strove,
Not vainly, to uplift it to the bright
      Portals of light.

Sunlight and shade dwell in the swaying trees,
Sunlight and shade and wind-sung melodies,
  Sunbeams and song ; but in my soul is night,
And moanings of a grief time doth not ease.
  The empty nest is ever in my sight,
And earthward faintly float sweet symphonies
    Upon the breeze.

THE VALEDICTORIAN.

Coral lip and budding bosom, rippling locks and
    eyes' coy shade
Whisper that behind her learning Cupid lies in
    ambuscade.

Gowned and happy, capped and hooded, radiant
    with the glow of youth,
Flute-voiced, like a bird full-throated, she upholds
    the cause of truth.

By the beard she plucks the greyheads, laughs
    to scorn the pride of man.
"Woman free is woman victor, let him rival her
    who can!"

Crying: "Woman shall have freedom;" crying:
    "Ceaseless be her strife
That, as unto man, be opened unto her the
    walks of life.

"Under foot man treads the animal: dies the ape,
    the tiger dies;
Man climbs upwards, seeking knowledge,
    shouldering through the centuries.

"Climbs the man and woman follows, yearning
    for the sunlit goal,
Yet he needs must thrust her downwards, her
    with like immortal soul;

"Thrust her down with brutal utterance: 'This
    and that is not for thee,
Keep thy kitchen, nurse thy children, leave the
    realm of thought to me.'

"Buoyant through the infinite æther, swings the
    world around the sun,
Blinded half by the other's shadow, else of darkness there were none.

"Let not man his selfish shadow cast upon the
    sister soul;
All is silence and desolation when the midnight
    shrouds the pole.

"Comes a cry from utter darkness, out of silence
    comes a wail,
Ignorance for light is pleading; surely succour
    shall not fail!

" Maiden-buds of woman-beauty, hot-housed by
    a father's love,
See the soul of man before them onward to perfection move.

" See, afar, the light of knowledge breaking on
    life's topmost height,
And with opening hearts and yearning bend
    towards it through the night.

" Wherefore bows the soul in worship, if there be
    no God to hear ;
Why doth woman yearn for knowledge if her
    mind be not man's peer?

" Freely woman plucks the blossoms in the
    shady dells that grow ;
On the maid, as on the stripling, Nature doth her
    gifts bestow.

" Sorrow's shafts nor winds of winter woman's
    beauty ever charms ;
Death spares not his torturing kisses when he
    takes her to his arms.

" Man hath many a mortal conflict, equal conflicts
    hath the maid,
Shall she not in equal armour for life's warfare
    be arrayed ?

"Grant the maid the shield of knowledge, gird
 the maid with learning's sword ;
Let her by man's side do battle with the powers
 that hate the Lord.

"Evil shuns the open sunlight, Ignorance a
 tyrant rules,
And the history of the future is determined in
 the schools."

Maiden bachelor, well you reason ; all your
 burning words are true,
And I see the chiefest reason man should heed
 your prayer—in you.

You are eager, you are kindly, knowledge dwells
 upon your lips ;
Natheless you are yet a woman, feminine to your
 finger tips.

"Nay, but"—flash man's eyes indignant,—"would
 she call me Ichabod ?
Would she drag me from mine eminence, she,
 the afterthought of God ?

THE VALEDICTORIAN. 41

"I am man; 'tis mine to follow all the beckoning
    shapes of life;
She is woman, and her duties lie in household,
    mother and wife.

"Unto man belongs the forum, unto man the
    desk and field,
Unto man the war with Nature to reveal the
    unrevealed,

"Massive head and stalwart shoulders, breast of
    bone and sinewy limb,
These are man's; shall frailer woman dare to
    enter lists with him!

"Shall the father bring forth children, shall they
    on his bosom lie
While, before the judge, the mother wrangles lest
    the murderer die?

"Mother! must man ever live to utter in a care-
    less breath
Mother, his first lisp in childhood; mother, his
    last cry in death?

"She that hacks the blackened body stolen from
    the kindlier tomb,
She that learning's fruit holds dearer than the
    fruitage of her womb;

"Leather-lunged and brazen-visaged, she, the sacred home that wrecks
On the reefs of vain ambition, shames her virtue, shames her sex.

"When man holds the moon at mid-day, like a cloud-wraith faint and white,
Nobler than the silver splendour of the harvest moon at night,

"He will hold the unsexed woman of the forum and the mart
Nobler than the stately matron reigning in his home and heart.

"Manhood is a storm-vext ocean, womanhood a rippling rill,
Which with sweet and sunny waters doth the bitter sea-heart fill.

"Man life's warrior is and victor, ever was and ever shall be
Woman's champion and provider; and his crowning solace she."

Stern my master, well you reason ; these your
 stormy words are true ;
Empress of the home is woman, warrior of the
 world are you.

Love will tame that fiery maiden eager now to
 rule the earth ;
Love will whisper her true kingdom at her help-
 less firstling's birth.

Youth is full of fire, and wisdom comes not
 instant with the hood ;
Aye, and man is fiery also, and a tyrant in his
 blood.

Wisdom is the fruit of knowledge, blossoming in
 the sun of years,
Rounding in the noon of life and ripening in a
 rain of tears.

Rare as golden sands is woman dowered with
 wisdom at her birth,
As Athena sprang full-statured, from the brain
 of Jove to earth.

One there is, and only one, of all the women I
 have known,
And she won me to a nature dimly mirroring
 her own.

Like a summer sunbeam gliding softly through
    a tangled grove,
Through the earthlier throng she wanders, and
    to see her is to love.

Perfect woman of perfect woman, helpful daughter,
    gentle bride,
Rules she all with unseen influence, as the fair
    moon rules the tide.

Like the harp, whose soul of music wakes responsive to the wind,
Wakes her soul to thrid thought's labyrinth,
    comrade of the husband mind.

Motherhood, nor cares of home her progress
    unto truth shall bar ;
Knowledge comes to such as she as to the twilight
    comes a star.

Genius soars on tireless pinions to the peaks of
    thought sublime,
Talent creeps, and meets a thousand cruel barriers
    in its climb.

Grant the woman-soul its wishes ; let the hosts
    of talent learn ;
Maids will choose the better husband, maids the
    sensual fool shall spurn.

Let them learn ; from perfect woman knowledge
shall not banish love,
And the cultured wife a helpmeet fitter for the
man shall prove.

Those whom God hath joined together act of
man may sunder not,
Fear to part the wife and husband by a barrier
of thought ;

Fear to have the woman only share the husband's lower life ;
Fear to hide his soul's true grandeur from that
kindred soul, his wife!

Nature hath no shameful secrets, let the maid
her pages scan
Fearlessly, though some, foolhardy, strive to
wrest his sword from man.

Woman may have need of woman ; purity
endureth much ;
From the rude sun shrinks the violet, yearning
for the dewdrop's touch.

Love rules not in every bosom ; let the maiden
choose between ;
Glimmering like the noonday moon and glowing
like the midnight queen.

Grant her choice, nor fear the issue; man will
 wed no unsexed maid;
Childless shall she die, and with her shall her
 sterile learning fade.

Man's heart in the breast of woman, what
 though such desert their trust,
Let not man, that weeds may perish, tread the
 golden grain to dust.

Fear no evil, all the beauties of the intellect and
 art
In true women cannot still the yearnings of the
 mother heart.

Open fling the doors of learning, all the wisdom
 maidens win
Some day shall the child that nestles at the
 mother's breast drink in.

Woman learns and man discovers; he is the
 pioneer of thought:
Yet in vain he strives and conquers if his
 children follow not.

Man is the promise of the present, woman of the
 years to be
When to manhood grows the prattler learning
 now upon her knee.

Woman stands at heaven's portals, at the gates of hell she stands ;
Wraps her silken tresses round us, leads us as with iron bands.

Priestess of our birth and burial, empress of our joy and pain,
Grant her knowledge, lest she drag us backward to the ape again.

THE LILACS AND THE STAR.

Through the dusk chambers of night,
  Paced by a sentinel star,
    Stealeth the soft-footed breeze,
Bearing sweet scents in its flight
  Out of a park where there are
    Nodding-plumed lilac trees.

Dimly the rays of the star,
  Glint in the whispering trees,
    Painting the blossoms with light.
Softly I hear from afar,
  Waked by the kiss of the breeze,
    Ripple of waves, through the night.

Sweet as the sweet-smelling trees,
  Filling the soul with delight,
    Love comes from such as you are.
Banished by you, swiftly flees
  Grief from my life, as at night
    Shades flee the sentinel star.

CHRISTMAS.

The church bells send their joyous chimes
    Across the snow-clad earth,
In token that in bygone times
    This day our Lord had birth.

The babe within a manger lay,
    And to it, from afar,
Came wise men, who, by night and day,
    Were guided by a star.

They knelt the humble cot beside,
    And costly presents made;
Then from the place in secret hied,
    Of Herod sore afraid.

The angels sang on Christ's birth-night
    To shepherds in the plain,
While all the sky was filled with light
    And echoed the refrain.

"Be peace on earth, goodwill to man,"
    Thus sang the angel throng,
And since the reign of Christ began
    Earth echoes that sweet song.

THE FLIRT.

If Time, the god of pleasure,
   If Time, the god of tears,
My moments would remeasure
   And give me back my years ;
Life's cup I would brim over,
   And all old pleasures drain ;
But the draught made me a lover
   I would not quaff again.

Like birds in summer bowers
   That trill their melody,
Hope sang, amid the hours,
   Its gladsome songs for me ;
Till, with her heartless beauty,
   She snared my thoughtless feet,
And love transcended duty,
   And life grew incomplete.

The bee that sips the flowers,
   Leaves golden pollen there,
And soon, in sunny hours,
   Ripe fruit the blossoms bear.

THE FLIRT.

From her soul might have fallen
    Love, my soul-bud upon,
And borne fruit, like the pollen,
    Ere was youth's summer done.

But, like the worm which settles
    Upon the white rose spray,
And slimes its satin petals,
    And eats its heart away,
She fastened on my weakness,
    And made my soul her prize,
And filled my life with bleakness,
    And ate my heart with lies.

She filled my life with sorrow,
    Then, laughing, flew away;
Mine was the woful morrow
    And hers the glad to-day.
The soul within her keeping
    Beneath her feet she trod,
Yet shall, some day, with weeping,
    Account for it to God.

LOVE AND A SERMON.

She loosed her close-coiled tresses,
    And to her feet they fell,
As over craggy nesses
    Streams plunge to ocean's swell.
Like wraiths on cloud-swept mountains,
    That robe a pine in storm,
Like mists on shapely fountains,
    So clung they to her form.

The Loreley that haunted
    The wild Teutonic stream,
And sweeter lyrics chaunted
    Than ever soul could dream,
No lovelier locks was combing
    To lure men to their doom,
Than those that, like a gloaming,
    Enwrapped the maid in gloom.

They glowed with hidden lustre,
    Like diamonds at night,
Or like a starry cluster
    That through the sky shines bright.

LOVE AND A SERMON.

They rippled o'er her shoulders
    And gleamed upon her breast,
As oft one sunbeam smoulders,
    At twilight, in the west.

Like any child, who lingers
    Some tempting spring beside
To thrust his eager fingers
    Within the eddying tide,
He stood beside the maiden,
    And toyed with each gold tress,
His heart with yearnings laden
    That tongue could scarce express.

Across his lips he drew them,
    And their soft shimmer kissed;
He added others to them,
    And bound them round his wrist;
He said: "As yearns the flower
    For dawn, I yearn for thee;
Thou hast me in thy power,
    What wilt thou do with me?"

She said: "If magic lurketh
    Within these locks of mine,
And in thy bosom worketh
    While round thy wrist they twine;

If in those heavy tresses,
   Across thy lips that lay,
My soul its wish expresses,
   What is there need to say?

" Thy lips shall be, forever,
   Truth's champions at need,
Thy hands their strength will never
   Shame by a ruthless deed;
The feet of all who stumble
   Thou shalt securely place,
And make thy proud soul humble
   Before the Throne of Grace."

A PAIR OF GEESE.

They're the veriest pair of geese I ever knew,
    Are these two,
As they nestle in the sunshine, wing to wing,
    Queen and King
Of an empire of delight, and of youth,
    Love and truth,
Her trustful eyes his grey eyes looking through,
    Hers are blue ;
While their elders hiss as loud as they dare
    At the pair.

Notwithstanding he's a goose, not a bird
    Ever heard,
Neither nightingale nor lark, no, nor thrush,
    Has so lush
A love song as his own, nor so choice,
    When his voice
For the sweet one at his side he doth raise
    In her praise—
Such a dainty little goose that she is,
    This of his.

Do the dullards honor him for his song?
        They are wrong;
Tis the goose and not the gander they should praise
            For the lays.
He's the harp and she's the harpist, and she brings
        From the strings
Strains that fill him with surprise that her art
        Should impart
To so ill-attuned a lyre melodies
        Such as these.

Yet this youthful pair of geese sometimes fight,
        Hiss and bite,
Over trifles light as air—not a few
        Lovers do,
For the sake of making up, I suppose,
        No one knows—
Yet woe to him who comes in between
        King and Queen,
For they'll peck him nigh to death ere they cease,
        Will these geese.

" And this loving pair of geese, who are they—
        Tell me, pray?"
Surely, Sweet, there is no need to tell who:
        One is you,
And the other . . pardon me? . . Do you not?
        Why, I thought
Love had shot your dear heart through . . You
      deny!
        So do I—
And there is but one poor goose, and my tale?
        What avail!

THE WOODBIRD.

A woodbird came to a maiden's cot,
    And chirped and cheeped and twittered and trilled,
For he was well content with his lot,
    And all the grove with his soul voice filled.

The bird was free as the fickle wind
    That lays its head in the violet's breast,
Then, laughing, springs from his couch to find
    Another bower in the aspen's crest;

Free as the scent of the dew-pearled rose,
    Free as the clouds that embrace the sky,
Free as the sun on the sea that glows,
    Free as the moonbeams, and not less shy.

Yet to the maiden's lone cot he came,
    And trilled and chirped and twittered and cheeped,
While she at him through the vine-clad frame
    Of her bright sun-fronting lattice peeped.

Her bosom laces the maid withdrew,
  And made her heart to the sunlight bare.
Into that nest the little one flew,
  And trilled and cheeped and was happy there.

Flew in and sang, and the passer-by,
  Weary and sad in the lonely grove,
Drew strength and joy from the melody,
  That oft-times broke with the weight of love.

TELL ME, DEAREST, WHY?

She's a young thing, and a sweet thing,
   Like a spray of Christmas holly;
She's a dear thing, and a neat thing,
   And I love her—is it folly?
Yet she fears me, and I tremble
   Like a leaf when she is nigh:
Tell me, why does Love dissemble;
   Tell me, dearest, why?

She's so merry and so kindly,
   And so gentle with all others;
Why will Love, then, act so blindly,
   Tell me why his fire he smothers?
Wherefore do I dwell in sorrow
   While joy hovers ever nigh;
Wherefore do I fear the morrow;
   Tell me, dearest, why?

I'm unworthy, that's no answer,
   Else to all men she's forbidden;
Love's a very necromancer,
   Finding worth where most 'tis hidden.

If she love me she will dower me
  With the worth the Fates deny ;
Wherefore, then, should fear o'erpower me,
  Tell me, dearest, why ?

I will hide my love no longer,
  All my heart I will discover,
I will say my soul grew stronger
  From the day it learnt to love her ;
Say my life is in her keeping,
  Say I wait for her reply ;
Darling, you are laughing, weeping ;
  Tell me, dearest, why ?

DEATH COMES TO US ALL.

Death comes to us all
  And bids man return
      Again to his God.
We are leaves, and we fall
      And mix with the sod ;
  But our spirits that yearn
  For the unknown, and burn
With vain hopes, naught can kill.

Mankind, like a rill
  To ocean that flows
      Through woodland and plain,
Makes his murmurings fill
      With a ceaseless refrain
  All the world as he goes,
  Till he finds his repose
In the depths of the grave.

'Twas ocean that gave
  The streamlet to earth,
      In the cycle of years
To return to its wave.
      God gave not for tears
  Us that soul, but for mirth ;
  To teach us life's worth ;
Then recalled it again.

LITTLE MISS BLUE EYES.

Little Miss Blue Eyes open the door,
  "Nobody's in," says she.
Little Miss Blue Eyes has evermore
  Stolen my heart from me.

Little Miss Blue Eyes stands at the door,
  "Will you come in?" asks she,
"Papa'll be back in an hour or more;"—
  Blue Eyes has seen through me.

Little Miss Blue Eyes opes her heart's door,
  "Nobody's in," says she.
(Would I might venture that threshold o'er
  Into its sanctity.)

Little Miss Blue Eyes, if you are kind,
  Keep me not at the door;
Into your love, from the cold and wind,
  Take me, dear, evermore.

Little Miss Blue Eyes stands at the door,
  Archly smiling at me:
"Papa'll be back in an hour or more,
  Come in and wait," says she.

IN LOVE'S BOWERS.

I am a bee in the bowers of love,
    Winging from red rose to lily.
Since woman is false, why should I not rove?—
    The love that is constant is silly.
            Who love only one,
            Of love may taste none;
            He who will rove
            Is never undone.

The sparkle that brightens the eye of Cerise,
    The folds of fair Alice's wimple,
And Lucy's lithe figure, my roving heart please
    As well as Kate's mouth or Nell's dimple.
            Who loves only one,
            Of love may taste none;
            He who will rove
            Is never undone.

Who loves only one may win beauty, I know,
  And a soul that is worth the possessing;
But if she's a blonde, why the brunettes must go,
  If brunette, the blondes lack his caressing.
            Who loves only one,
            Of love may taste none;
            He who will rove
            Is never undone.

It gives me no pang that my Alice in pain
  Sees Cerise have a share of my kisses,
And Lucy may pout, and sweet Nell, in disdain,
  Turn away when my worship she misses.
            Who loves only one,
            Of love may taste none;
            He who will rove
            Is never undone.

I care not a whit; there are maids fair as they—
  I leave reconcilement to lovers—
The honey I've sipped, so I wander away—
  Oh! happy is life to the rovers.
            Who loves only one,
            Of love may taste none;
            He who will rove
            Is never undone.

IN EXILE.

Though friends and fortune smile, this is not
    home ;
No dews of peace on me, constrained to roam,
  Drop these strange skies, my sad soul bending
    over,
From their flame-fretted, silent, soulless dome ;
  No sun-throned days, warm as a maiden lover,
Bring rest, though they be sweet as wild bees'
    comb,—
        This is not home.

This is not home : my spirit in exile
Faints for old scenes. Dear argent-girdled isle,
  Loved birthplace, rising, Venus-like, from
    foam,
Like her, thou slav'st me with thy beauty's wile.
  In absence still the crags my feet have clomb,
The mountain grove and ferny, cool defile
        My heart beguile.

IN EXILE.

This is not home : Beside her cold hearthstone,
Amid the glooms of age, one sits alone,
   Nor turns to welcome with a mother's smile
The nestling from her bosom now far flown.
  Naught can her heart to its loss reconcile,
And for the gentle nest it once had known,
       My heart makes moan.

This is not hóme : no longer at my side
She stands, whom God hath promised for my bride,
   Her love-deep eyes upglancing to my own.
No place is home where is my heart denied
  Her smile, in whose pure sunshine it has grown—
Love, ere I thee forsook, to wander wide,
       Would I had died !

NOT NATURE, BUT MAN.

Not for me do the song birds lilt in the meadows,
    Or slide through the tree-tops;
Not for me do the sunshowers harry their shadows
    With pattering raindrops.

Not for me do the wheat fields dip to the breezes
    That over the wolds blow;
Not for me does the murmuring brook as it pleases
    Through slumberous vales flow.

Not for me is the scream that breaks from the shingle
    Dragged down by the fierce sea;
Not for me does the violet bloom in the dingle
    Beneath the gnarled oak tree.

I know but the sights and strange sounds of the city,
    The stony-faced buildings,
The unceasing tumult of feet, and the ditty
    The beggar for bread sings.

On my ear falls the clamor of trade, and the rattle
    Of carts in the roadway,
The voices of innocent babes, as they prattle
    At this and at that play.

The songs that I hear are the hymns of the nations,
    Not strains that the birds sing ;
The wings I see flutter are man's aspirations
    That him nearer God bring.

The groves that I dream in are street lamps that glitter
    Mist-veiled, through the night air,
The ocean I look on is life's ocean, bitter
    With joys that float dead there.

The wind that bows down the ripe heads in my meadows
    With sudden and chill breath,
And harries the clouds in pursuit of their shadows
    By mortals is called Death.

Not nature but man is best theme of the poet,
    And oft though my song breaks,
I sing of man's soul, yet alas, who may know it,
    Save Him who the soul makes?

TO HER LOVER.

Sweet is your worship, dearest, to my heart,
  I love to know you mine, both soul and body,
And hate the world that gladly would us part,
  Luring your love with flaunting joys, and gaudy.

But do I lead you nearer unto God,
  My love, who say so ardently you love me?
Am I your highest aim—a pretty clod—
  Or does your spirit rise through mine, above me?

Is pity quickened: is your soul at strife
  With wrong, and grown enamored of perfection?
What new thoughts, hopes, sensations fill your life?—
  Thus would I try the gold of your affection.

Are you content, love, or do you aspire
  From arm-zoned joys of earth to joys supernal?
For love is never love if its wings tire
  Short of the glorious throne of the Eternal.

THE FLOWER GIRL.

She is a stately golden rod,
   Crowned with her sunny hair,
And her eyes are like twin violets,
   Her lips like roses rare.

The lily's bloom is on her cheeks,
   Sweeter her breath than thorn,
And her voice is as the stir of buds
   That greet the wind of morn.

The flowers she wreathes have odors rich,
   Their hues are soft and gay,
But the graces of her maiden soul
   More dainty are than they.

TO A COQUETTE.

I hate you for the power you wield
    Over my foolish heart.
I hate you, since you make me yield,
    A captive to your art.

I hate your glorious eyes, that shine
    With joy and virtue fraught.
I hate your golden locks, that twine
    About my every thought.

I hate you, for you make me love
    The very ground you tread.
I hate you—since I cannot move
    Your heart with mine to wed.

A SONG.

Who would not brave the fiercest storm
   That ever shook a rafter,
If but to know the sweetened charm
   Of the calm that follows after!

Who would not face the darkest night
   That ever followed even,
If but to take renewed delight
   In the glowing noonday heaven!

Who would not quarrel with his love
   And brave the storm of sorrow,
If only love's bright bliss to prove
   With kisses on the morrow!

INTIMACY.

Friend, each knows other to the very heart's core,
  Reads thoughts in eyes before the tongue can voice them,
Knows, as a singer knows his studied part's score,
  The feelings' range, what grieves and doth rejoice them.

Between us naught is new. Thou dost but find me
  An empty shell that tells the same tale ever;
Thou of a favorite poem dost remind me,
  Whose pages well I know, and need turn never.

This is the woe of life, to reach the limit
  Of the soul's kingdom in the heart that rules us—
The breath that shows the mirror glass doth dim it;
  'Tis what we wish, not what we have, that schools us.

THE COURIER DE BOIS.

My home is in the forest shade,
   My rifle is my bride,
From whom not e'en the fairest maid
   Can lure me to her side.

My bed is on the scented pines,
   My coverlet the sky,
Yet not the King himself reclines
   On sweeter couch than I.

Soundly we slumber, till the dawn
   Breaks in a flood of gold
O'er forest dense and dewy lawn,
   The mountain and the wold..

And then I rise, and with my bride
   Thread the awakening wood;
And woe the savage beast betide
   That breaks our solitude.

ISCARIOT.

Hush thee! hush! he may be in heaven
    For aught we know. Did he not repent;
And is it not said who repents is forgiven?
    His pardon, then, there may naught prevent·

He knew that Christ was, indeed, the Lord!
    And what of that; did not Jesus say
'Twas he should do that deed so abhorred,
    However could he escape fate, pray?

Christ he betrayed, and he shortly went
    And told the priests their gold had a stain,
And proffered it back, not a farthing spent
    Of that he had bartered his soul to gain.

They would not take it: he let it lie,
    Blood-money cast at their guilty feet;
And wandered forth, in despair, to die,—
    Why say his repentance was incomplete?

COME DOWN TO THE SHADE.

Come down to the shade, my beautiful maid,
    Come down to the shade of the wood ;
The whip-poor-will calls on the edge of the glade,
    Frogs dreamily flute by the flood.

The moon saileth high through the warm starry sky,
    A wheeling hawk screams in the night,
A ribbon of silver, the stream eddies by,
    And rustles the reeds in its flight.

Sleep's finger is laid on the lips of the glade,
    Alone by the river I brood ;
Come down to the shade, my beautiful maid,
    Come down to the shade of the wood.

LOVE.

Love is the bitterest pleasure upon earth,
  The keenest purgatory of mankind.
It kindles fires of hope on the heart's hearth ;
  Only to quench them utterly, and blind
  To the youth-conjured dreams of bliss the mind,
And Jealousy crowns king, who makes the smile
  Of woman—by God to comfort man designed—
To the crazed lover seem hell's deepest guile
With which she lures all men into subjection vile.

And yet when once the words of love are spoken,
  Soul vows exchanged, and on red lips and warm
Is pressed of love the burning seal and token,
  No longer heard is Jealousy's alarm,
  And earth revibrates to the new-found charm,
Hope towers to heaven, Despair in death low lies;
  Heart beats on heart, and, trustful, fears no harm ;
A brighter sun is shining in the skies,
And earth seems earth no more, but rather Paradise.

THE MAIDEN'S SONG.

A home in a far-off city,
  A room in that distant home,
There singeth a maid a ditty
  Of a lover, who doth not come.

Her eyes, like the stars adorning
  The evening sky, flash bright,
Then are veiled in mist, like Morning,
  That weeps at the tomb of Night.

" He will come to my arms to-morrow ; "—
  But to-morrow he doth not come.
" Is it sweet to Thee, God, my sorrow ? "
  Then the faltering lips are dumb.

TO ROSE.

The names are changed, dear Rose;
   New France is now the Old:
For here among the ice and snows
   Time's flood has scarcely rolled.

Old France has lost the lays
   It loved in olden time;
But these sweet songs of other days
   Still linger in our clime.

Still may we hear them sung
   By many a peasant maid,
As with her heart upon her tongue,
   She wanders through the glade.

We hear them still when glows
   The moon in flowery dells,
And when, across the sparkling snows,
   Ring out the jingling bells.

Their simple notes we hear
  Around the blazing hearth.
At will they summon up the tear,
  Or fill the heart with mirth.

Nor shall we e'er repine
  That time has left us young,
While by sweet lips as red as thine
  These antique songs are sung.

MIND AND BODY.

Mind and body, warp and woof,
    With each other are entwined,—
Body living, not aloof,
    Living not aloof the mind.

Force and matter, what they are
    To each other, so are these,
As its light is to a star,
    Organ to its melodies.

Quench the steady-burning light,
    Vanishes the star we see
Into interstellar night;
    From existence, it may be.

Still the organ, what remains,
    Save the metal and the wood?
Silent are the heavenly strains,
    Lost in empty solitude.

Brother, rule the restless mind,
    That like starlight it may shine;
Rule the body, lest you find
    Hushed the melody divine.

SONNETS.

TO LOUISE.

Louise, thy stately name sounds in my ear
  Like a sea wave, that, gathering, hill on hill,
  Upon the blue horizon, smooth and still,
Sweeps to the shore, and as it draws anear,
Breaks silence, foaming thunders, clarion-clear,
  Up the sloped strand, and with its voice doth fill
  The vaulted sky, that shakes with sudden thrill,
While other sounds hold breath, the psalm to hear.

In me thy name makes dumb all trivial things,
  Dear maid with lily soul. Who would aspire
  To enter thy heart's palace, even as friend,
Must rise, like thee, upon angelic wings,
  Ever to noblest thoughts and deeds, and bend
  His vision Godward with youth's passionate fire.

ALBANI.

How many thoughts man hath speech cannot
   voice!
  How many dim reflections of the sky
    There are, whose shapes elude our mortal eye!
What spirit songs man hears! what deep soul joys
He knows, whose thrill his life's glad calm annoys
    For utterance in grand words that cannot die!
    Ah! these reveal that souls shall death defy,
And must for immortality make choice.

  Yet not so cruel is Heaven that it gives
    No language for these cravings of the soul.
  In melody the soul's soul speaks and lives,
    Ruling all hearts with its divine control;
      And in thy song, Albani, utterance find
    The else dumb secrets of all human kind.

IN THE MORNING.

Sleep's bride, upon her spotless couch she lay,
  In one hand's dainty nest her cheek, dream-flushed,
  For spake by night thoughts that by day were hushed.
Smiles round her mouth's ripe rose, like bees, did play,
Or like, in the east, the first coy beams of day;
  And in the tresses her pure brow that brushed
  Were yet the roses, faded now and crushed,
Had crowned her in the hours of revelry.

  Gently her bosom heaved, and one nude arm,
    Whose goddess-grace no marble could excel,
  Fronted the rising Sun, whose glances warm
    Upon its unconcealèd beauty fell;
      And as the lord of day the pure flesh kissed,
        He touched with flame my love-gift on her wrist.

I HAD BEEN LIKE A SHIP.

I had been like a ship upon the sea,
  By flying gleams at midnight led astray,
  And following ever, found them melt away
In utter void and bleak obscurity.
A rush of waters well nigh whelmèd me,
  And I scarce dreamed to see another day;
  Yet labored on, hope lost and wild dismay
Through rope and canvas shrilling in loud glee.

  Then, like the steadfast light upon the shore,
    Trimmed in the window by the waiting wife
      To guide the trawlers home, thee in the night
  I saw; and suddenly the tempest's roar
    Was hushed, the waves grew calm, the clouds took flight,
    And all was peace upon my sea of life.

THE ETERNITY OF LIFE.

Where, in an ancient temple of the East,
  Before rude carvings kneel idolators,
  Along the roof a cloud of incense pours
From a huge fane ; and by the fire a priest
Stands mummering on fresh faggots: nor has ceased,
  For years one numbers by the hundred scores
  Of those that once knelt on the foot-worn floors,
The fire to burn in honor of some beast.

  Priestess of Life is Nature, and its fire
    Mysterious she feeds with flesh. Forms die,
      Yet Life dies never. Like the ruddy flames,
  Which burn forever on the pagan pyre,
    Life changes but its shape; what life have I
      Long æons since quickened ancestral frames.

THE PEARL BRACELET.

I.

The Vision of Beauty.

Love knew her beautiful; and yet that night
  Truth limned her than my fancy's dreams more fair.
Blithely, she moved towards me, up the stair,
Vestured in opal, while the steadfast light
Glowed on smooth arms and bosom lily-white,
  Like sun on gems. Before that vision rare
  Of loveliness I stood, my heart in snare,
She proud, yet shamed to have so tranced my sight.

  Meseemed her soul had reached its angel flower,
    Though still she dwelt in this death-gated land.
    Soul-stricken by her radiant purity,
I faltered words, forgotten to this hour,
    And bending low, with deep humility,
  Kissed the warm whiteness of her ungloved hand.

II.

THE BRACELET.

To deck her child, the richest of white roses
  Nature had culled. As Nature's vicar, I
  Wreathed them with fern, and while the maiden shy
Stood smiling on me, pinned the happy posies
In her soft gown, where, as the wave discloses
  The pearly shells that on the shore-edge lie,
  The lace foamed back and showed the ivory
Of that dear nest wherein arch Love reposes.

  She bound three rosebuds in her shimmering hair;
    Then gloved her arms, and held them out to me,
      Eyes veiled. I clasped the bracelet on her wrist,
  Gold and five pearls, and bade her see it there.
    She looked and blushed, and, shyly, for my fee,
      Proffered her lips, whose rosiness I kissed.

III.
Her Promise.

"Pearls, set with gold," she murmured; "once again
  Thou givest me pearls. See! in thy ring I wear
  Are pearls, like dew tangled in golden hair.
I love them, being thine, yet now am fain
To love them less, that these some love may gain
  Thou givest me now, thy newer gift and rare.
  Oh, what am I, that thou canst think me fair,
And my weak soul on soul of thine sustain!

"Pearls! dear they say that pearls betoken tears,—
  How old-folk fancies cling about us still!
    Thou wilt not, Love, bring any tears to me?
  Yet if thou shouldst, and Fate's cup-bearing years
    Brimful of grief our mutual goblet fill,
      Whate'er thou drinkest I will drink with thee."

THE BLIND STREET FIDDLER.

He sits amid the ceaseless ebb and flow
  Of human life, in multitudes alone,
  And listens to their ceaseless monotone.
His sightless eyes see never to and fro
The hurrying waves in divers eddies go;
  See not the shadows on that ocean thrown
  By cliff-like, mocking walls of voiceless stone
Which shore the restless tides that sweep below.

  Among them, yet not one of them, sits he
    And sends his clear-toned music over all,
      Charming the waves to music as they roll.
  Even thus great thoughts sweep over life's vast sea,
    Along the shores of time, and the waves fall
      And rise in rhythm under their control.

HOW SHALL I PAINT THEE?

How shall I paint thee, my belovèd one,
  Or feeble words of mine depict thy soul,
  Whose radiant beauty is my being's goal!
Thou art like some fair creature of the sun,
Tissued of light. Fit word has language none
  To picture thee. Not Shelley's hyperbole,
  Nor even of Milton the sonorous roll
Might justice to thy glorious charms have done.

  And though to paint thee there were fitting pen,
    No canvas might receive such tints sublime.
    Yet painted in true colors, Lou, thou art,
  Not by my hand, most humble among men,
    But with a diamond, for all future time,
      By Love, upon the adamant of my heart

CHRIST WAS NO IDLER IN LUXURIOUS HALLS.

To laboring shepherds, watching by their sheep,
  The Angels first the glorious news revealed
    Of Jesus' birth. Their heavenly anthems pealed
To gladden men who toiled while earth did sleep.
A humble carpenter the child did keep
  Till manhood. Those who first by Jesus kneeled
  Were laborers. To labor in God's field
He chose the toilers of the land and deep.

  Christ was no idler in luxurious halls ;
    He shared the life and trials of the poor
      And gave them comfort. Wherefore on this day,
  That to all men His day of birth recalls,
    Should every toiler upon earth be gay,
  Thinking of Him who did their life endure.

NIGHT THOUGHTS.

How calm the summer night is! In no tree
  Whispers a leaf. The stars that pace the skies,
  Night's picket-watch on Day, blink their bright eyes,
As though they keep their watch but sleepily.
The city sleeps and murmurs dreamily,
  And o'er the trees I see the moon arise,
  Full-orbed, and mark its glance of mild surprise
That I should scorn Oblivion's clemency.

  Wherefore should I these hours of torment know?
    All nature sleeps, and hath from thought surcease;
    Yet my sad thoughts a weary vigil keep,
  Till, like the full-orbed moon, before me, lo!
    My radiant love appears to bring me peace;
    And murmuring her dear name I sink to sleep.

TO THE SEA.

Awestruck, I stand on thy resounding shore,
  O deep, tumultuous, world-encircling Sea!
  Meet symbol of God's vast eternity.
Ere yet earth's womb a living creature bore,
As thou art now, thou wast, and thy hoarse roar
  Shook the void air. Nature directing thee,
  Thou didst map out the continents to be,
Make and unmake and build them up once more.

  Gigantic saurians sported in thy waves,
    Lived centuries out, and to oblivion sank;
      Beside thee grew strange plants, that are forgot;
  Earth-shaking beasts thy tributaries drank,
  And died, and lie in undiscovered graves:
      Yet thou hast ebbed and flowed, and altered not.

IF YOU SHOULD DIE.

If you should die, who stole away my soul,
  And, nestling where it dwelt, its loss conceal,
  Whose virtue is the shrine at which I kneel,
Whose praises are my labor's utmost goal;
If you should pass away, nor more control
  The thoughts I think, the joys and griefs I feel;
Then would the fountains of my life congeal;
Death be a friend whose kind touch makes me whole.

'Twas your eyes taught me sight; your ears, to hear;
  Your tongue, soft speech; your grace and goodness, God;
    Your trust, my weakness; and if you should die,
  Then were I nothing but a soulless clod,
Dumb, blind and deaf, barren of laugh and tear,
    Half doubting if there rules a God on high.

ANTICIPATION AND REALIZATION.

The bud, wherein slumbers the perfect flower,
  The acorns, in whose cells the vast oaks rest,
  The fledgelings, chirping in their secret nest,
Wind-rocked, far up in some aerial bower,
The sun, new-born at day-dawn's purple hour,
  The child, close-cuddled to its mother's breast,
  Thrill the glad soul with hope; for they suggest
Completeness Time shall give them yet for dower.

  Sweet are the joys anticipation brings;
    Yet sweeter far the realization is.
  The man excels the child, the fledged bird sings
    The blithest song, the flower hath daintier charms
    Than any bud; and all youth's dreams of bliss
      Have been surpassed in one another's arms.

FEAR NOT TO DO RIGHT.

With thy pure heart thou hast scant need from me
  Of friendly council. Thou art like a flower
  That fronts the glowing sun, and, hour by hour,
Follows its course, and even dreamily,
In darkest night, turns that its face may be
  To earliest dawn. Thou hast been given the power
  To see the dawn of truth from thy soul's tower,
While gropes the world in night's profundity.

  Yet, since thou wilt have counsel, having fear
    Of this bad world's derision of good deeds,
      Then, that no evil thou may'st ever rue,
  Let this brief sentence to thy heart lie near,
    To nerve it for thy life's extremest needs,
      Do ever that thou art afraid to do!

WHY A BRIDE WEEPS.

Well may, when wed, the love-crowned bride
 shed tears,
 For she has said farewell to her old life
 To venture for love's sake into the strife
Of worldly matters, nor in after years
Again shall have her girlhood's lack of fears.
 With watching and sad cares the world is rife,
 And she has taken up Fate's burden as wife,
Trusting in him whom love to her endears.

 How wonderful the spell of love must be
 That maids will bid farewell to what has
 been,
 And trust themselves to one for his love's
 sake,
Confronting Death's stern visage fearlessly.
 Oh! youth, thus dowered by love, pray
 God to make
You worthy of the priceless soul you win.

THE NOBLEST POEM.

Pride hath no shelter in a poet's breast,
  Though he may find his words on every
    tongue,
  For well he knows, though sweet the song he
    sung,
Still is his heart's ideal unexpressed.
A few stray gems he gathers from the best
  The treasures of his intellect among,
  Nor has done more, when his scant pearls are
    strung,
Than dimly what his fancy grasped, suggest.

  The noblest thoughts expression cannot find
    In any tongue, for language flies too low
      To reach the mount which thought's first
        day-streak greets.
      There was a greater Shakespeare than we
        know,
      A grander Milton, a diviner Keats:
  The noblest poem is the poet's mind.

MY LADY.

To see her in the world a man would think
  Her chaste and beautiful, yet call her cold,
  And turn for love to one of softer mould,
Whose lips beg kisses, and whose glances drink
Deep draughts of joy at passion's treacherous brink.
  Yet they misjudge, whose lips, thus overbold
  Cry that her thoughts nor love nor passion hold
Because from their caress her soul doth shrink.

I have seen love touch that calm face with flame,
  Set those proud lips to suing, ay, and melt
    Those haughty eyes to tenderness, that now
    So steadfast shine beneath that snowy brow;
And I have heard her murmur one dear name
At morn, when at her orisons she knelt.

THE TRUE IMMORTALS.

All men are heritors of noble thought,
   Co-workers in all acts that are divine.
   The visions of a Plato, they are thine;
With Newton thou the thoughts of God hast sought;
Thy blood the triumph of just strifes has bought;
   Around thy brows the wreaths of Petrarch twine:
Woven is the past with thy new life and mine,
For noblest thoughts can never be forgot.

   Man is a shadow in time's sunlit way,
      A wild wood rose, that blossoms, fades and dies.
   Born with the dawn, at dusk he fades away.
      Actions and thoughts outlast the centuries
   And hold eternity itself at bay,—
      They only are life's true realities.

THE PANTHEIST.

He knows the name of every creeping thing,
  Of every plant in all the country round,
  And when and in what haunts it may be found.
To name a bird he needs but hear it sing.
He speculates how long it took a wing
  To evolve and lift an eagle from the ground;
  And scorning miracles, doth priests astound,
Saying Nature's laws admit no altering.

  He reads the mystic story of the past
    In hill and vale and rock, and says all life
      Is one, and flees from form to form from
        death;
  And man himself but part is of a vast
    And universal energy, a breath
Of one great *Am*, with Nothingness at strife.

IN THE CANOE.

I.

Dost thou recall that evening thou and I
  Together in our eggshell bark took flight
  Upon the noiseless lake? How dark that night!
Though many a star was glowing in the sky!
Under the leafage slept the shadows shy,
  Until the zephyrs stole, with footsteps light,
  Among them, and embraced them, lost to sight
Of curious eyes beneath earth's canopy.

  I saw thee like a shadow in the prow;
    I saw the flashing of thy hand, that trailed
      Half in the tide; I watched thy night-veiled face,
  Whose thoughtful eyes, beneath thy tressy brow,
    Shone on my soul: and then the starlight paled,
      And mine eyes saw but thee in all that space.

II.

In all that waste of waters we alone
  Were floating. Save that from the shore there gleamed
A golden lamplight, all the great world seemed
Afar from us. Methought that we had flown—
Buoyed on the æther sea by power unknown—
  Up to the gates of heaven; and then I dreamed
Those were an angel's eyes that on me beamed
With love that was but mirroring my own.

  Great thoughts, high aspirations thronged my mind,
    The nobleness of duty grew more clear.
  With thy pure soul my soul seemed intertwined,
    Like two pure flames that mingle at one fane.
  Oh! wherefore, love, when heaven to us was near,
    Did we two ever seek the earth again?

SONNETS AT NIAGARA.

I.

First Feelings.

Who can conceive the feelings of the first
  Fond hearts that, wandering hitherward by night,
  From uncongenial camp fires taking flight
To Solitude, saw on their vision burst
These wondrous falls in rolling mist-wrack hearsed,
  And felt the thunder of plunging waters smite
  Their ears and drown their murmurs of delight,—
Ah! who can dream what mutual thought they nursed?

  Since then have fallen athwart the brink of Time
    Years multitudinous as the hurrying waves
    That leap Niagara's gulf, yet thou and I
    Here standing where the latest ripple laves
  The rock ere dashing to its death sublime,
    Of those first lovers know the ecstacy.

II.
LOVE'S CHANGEABLENESS.

How many heart-wed lovers here have stood,
  Like us, beside Niagara's folding brink,
  Watching the thirsty gorge the torrent drink!
How many, like ourselves, in solitude,
Have stood above the fierce, moon-smitten flood,
  Through whose mist clouds a myriad star points twink,
  And felt the grandeur of the cataract sink
Into their souls until was thought subdued!

  Here many human hearts have throbbed with love,
    And dreamed their love would live beyond the grave,
    Strong as Niagara's rush, deep as its fall,
  Only within a little space to prove
    Their love as changing as the tumbling wave
      Which breaks in mist that darkly shadows all.

III.

LOVE'S BLINDNESS.

Little we knew when by the thund'rous tide
  We stood and looked into its depths profound,
  Where boiled the waters after their fierce bound
Over the cliff that doth the streams divide,
Upper from nether, what of Fate did hide
  The veil, or that the voice of Love should sound
  In our ears and earth's discordancy be drowned,
And souls unite, leaping the wall of pride.

  Little thou thoughtst that love was in the air,
    Touching thy turbulent curls, thy flushing cheek,
      Blue eyes, dear heart, and slumbering on thy lips.
  Little I knew boy-love was buried there,
    And man's affection deathless, strong, yet meek,
      Woke at the calling of the water drips.

IV.
AT THE SISTER ISLANDS.

We stand upon the bridge and look below
  Into the rush of waters, streaking white
  Along the sunken rocks, so swift their flight;
And while we look, it seems to us as though
We move, and the quick tides have ceased to flow.
  So much the motion juggles with our sight,
  That we must lift, to see the truth aright,
Our faces to the sky's unclouded glow.

  Thus man may stand on truth while error sweeps
    Beneath him to its misty overthrow
  Into the tumult of the nether deeps;
    Yet, self deceived, often the soul will cry:
    "Error is truth, and truth is falsity,"
  Until a God-ward glance the truth doth show.

V.
The Whirlpool.

After the leaps tumultuous of the tides
  That through the narrow, rocky canyon surge,
  With sudden sweeps over some ledge's verge
That underneath the seething waters hides,
With clash of snow-plumed billows on all sides,
  That like strong warriors ceaseless combat urge,
Niagara's waves in one another merge,
Where, calmly deep, the circling whirlpool glides.

  Thus is it with our love: the earliest sweep
    Of feeling was tumultuous, and the soul
      Of each was torn and tossed; but now, at last,
      Of love the stormy rapids have been passed,
  And we are in the whirlpool, that will keep
    Our lives forever in its calm control.

BE THINE OWN IMAGE BUILDER.

Be thine own image builder, nor have fear
  To overthrow the idols of past days.
    Test all by thine own touchstone; Truth displays
Her beauty in the light of doubt most clear.
To be a Man thy Maker sent thee here;
  Then swerve not from thy truth, fall blame or praise
On thee from fools who follow in the ways
Of pilot minds. In all things be sincere.

  There is none other wholly like to thee;
    Thou hast a task none other man may do,
      Nor canst thou do it if thou dost not wage
    Eternal strife with all thou think'st untrue,
      Be faithful to thyself, and of thine age
Thou shalt become the grand epitome.

HEART HUNGER.

Oh! Love, to press thy bosom to my own,
  To lose my lips among the tress and tress
  That touch thy brow with many a soft caress,
And reap a score where one love glance was sown,
To stand before thy soul's majestic throne,
  Nor find thee, as to others, pitiless;
  That only for this draught of wretchedness,
Fate-forced I drink in exile, can atone.

  Nor day nor night brings peace since we twain parted.
    By day I but lament my joyless plight;
      And when I dream, and find thee at my side,
  And waking, seek thee, still my love is thwarted,
    For cruel darkness tears thee from my sight,
      And vainly grope my void arms for my bride.

DANTE TO BEATRICE.

I care not though I may not mate with thee,
  For, natheless, I have made thee all my own ;
  And henceforth thou shalt evermore be known,
And rescued from Oblivion's hungry sea,
As one to whom a poet bent the knee.
  Let whom thou wilt reign with thee on Love's throne,
  In death I will sit there with thee alone,
And all the world shall speak of thee and me.

  What though thou givest him thy body and soul !
    Thou canst not rob me of the soul I love ;
    It is but the creation of my mind,
  And cannot ever pass from my control.
    Save mine, all eyes to thy true soul are blind,
  And it shall share with me the life above.

CUPID AND PSYCHE.

I.

CUPID TO PSYCHE.

I touch, yet cannot see thee, and mine eyes
  Draw their fringed veils athwart them, that they may
Again, in fancy, see thy majesty.
Thy wealth of tresses on my shoulder lies;
I feel thy bosom melting into sighs;
  Coyly around my neck thy white arms stray,
  Drawing my face to thine, and I obey,
Till lips meet lips and make their sweets a prize.

  We are far from earth and earthliness, we twain,
    And feed each on the other's rapid breath;
      To heart-beat answers heart-beat, soul to soul,
  And, overmastered by my love, I strain
    Thee in mine arms. Would that the years might roll,
  Nor ever part us more in life or death.

II.
PSYCHE TO CUPID.

In bondage sweet of love thy slave am I,
  And have no will, but to be loved by thee,
  My lips are parched for kisses, feed thou me,
Surely these rubies yet one kiss can buy?
I am all thine, nor can thee aught deny;
  And shouldst thou tire of me and set me free,
  Like bird released from long captivity,
Cageward my heart would flutter back, or die.

  I have withheld nor body, nor my soul;
    Thou hast awakened with thy passionate kiss
      The love that slumbered on my ignorant lips.
  Right, wrong, life, death, keen sorrow or deep bliss,
  I know not—care not—which may be my goal,
    For in thine arms all thought from my heart slips.

A MOTHER'S THOUGHT.

Once a frail toddler at her mother's knee,
  Uplifting her blue eyes to that calm face,
  Sweet mirrors to reflect love's perfect grace;
Once a shy maid, all ideality,
Dreaming the world as innocent as she;
  Once blushing in her lover's fond embrace,
  And weeping farewell to her nesting-place
To walk with him towards eternity:

  To-day within the palace of the wood,
    Whose roof is intricate with many a scroll
      Of shifting sun, with her own babe she
        strays,
  Tasting the joys of happy motherhood,
    Yet grave for thinking, even as she plays,
  Herself the mother of a deathless soul.

AT THE RECITAL.

Midway we sate between the nave and door,
  Between the worldly tumult of the street
  And the calm silence of God's pure retreat.
We heard the lofty organ pipes outpour
Their mighty waves of music. More and more
  The melody encompassed us. The sweet
  Tones roused my soul to know life incomplete,
A wave of music dashing on death's shore.

  Midway between the world and God we sate,
    While through the church the Spirit of Music stole,
      And in its robes harmonic wrapped us twain.
  Of thy pure soul, from evil free and hate,
    Then woke my heart to hear the grand refrain,
      And yearned to reach, like thee, life's noblest goal.

HEINE'S THREE KISSES.

I.

THE GREEK GODDESS.

Through leafy boughs the summer moonbeams sift
  Upon a shattered column, wreathed with flowers,
  By which, like some bright vision of dream hours,
A sculptured goddess lies, her bosom's drift,
When curious winds the jealous blossoms lift,
  Glowing amid the grasses' dew-pearled bowers.
  Sleeping she seems, for night's kind genius dowers
The marble with life's flush as his love gift.

  Beside the statue kneels a child, and bends
    To lay his lips upon the Parian cheek,
      And kiss the stately brow and pulseless breast,
    Which yield him, for the warmth his young cheek lends,
      Visions of beauty, which, in futile quest,
    He evermore throughout the world shall seek.

II.
RED SEFCHEN.

Youth and the sword blood-drunken, that hath drunk
  An hundred lives and is insatiate,—
  Youth and the sword, and Beauty, that doth wait
The embrace;—ripe lips, whose smiles would lure a monk;
Fair flesh, fire-flaming locks, like sun half sunk,
  Glowing in clouds, through evening's crimson gate,
  Tempt him to love. He challenges his fate,
Nor has she from his burning kisses shrunk.

Meet was it that beneath the thirsting sword
  Himself into Red Sefchen's arms he flung,
    For Innocence then learned the love of guilt
  And passion's brand, above his head long swung,
    In his young soul was buried to the hilt,
Nor ever was a richer flood outpoured.

III.

THE VENUS OF MILO.

The panting rabble of the Paris street
  Give him no heed, but round him surge and
    roar,
  A grief-aged man, a cynic at death's door,
And drive him to the Louvre's calm retreat.
There, as he stands bewildered, his eyes meet
  The Venus Victrix, and he falls before
  That radiant Beauty-vision, weeping sore,
And prints a kiss upon her naked feet.

  Through years of grief and passion he had
    sung
    The praises of the vision of his youth,
  Till with his music all the world had rung,
    Only to find, at last, when death was
      near,
    That vision of soul beauty and sweet truth
      Still graspless in the marble form appear.

EPILOGUE.

I stood one evening on a rocky coast,
  Beneath my feet the jetsam of the sea,
  Amid the tide-smoothed sands, and over me,
From burly-chested rocks, the salt spray tossed,
Threatening the empire that the waves had lost;
  And as I looked, quenched seemed the Sun
    to be,
  Yet for a space there lingered happily,
One ray, the last of Day's majestic host.

  Louise, thou standest on my fancy's shore,
    Amid the jetsam of thy lover's verse,
      The tide withdrawn, and evening closing
        down.
  The Sun has set, perchance to rise no more,
    Yet still the skies one lingering sunbeam
      nurse,
      That smiles on thee in kindness ere 'tis
        flown.

www.ingramcontent.com/pod-product-compliance
Lightning Source LLC
Chambersburg PA
CBHW021940160426
43195CB00011B/1169